WITHDRAWN

UNIVERSITY COLLEGE CHICHESTER LIBRARIES

AUTHOR:

GISLER.

TITLE:

ART

DATE:

JUNE 2002

SUBJECT:

ARD.

D0492854

ART

Maria Gisler

VGM Career Horizons
NTC/Contemporary Publishing Company

Library of Congress Cataloging-in-Publication Data

Gisler, Maria.
　　Art / Maria Gisler.
　　　　p.　　cm. — (VGM's career portraits)
　　Summary: Examines career opportunities in painting, sculpting,
photography, museums, art galleries, and teaching. Includes
interviews of persons working in art fields, success stories, tips,
and suggestions.
　　ISBN 0-8442-4382-5
　　1. Art—Vocational guidance—United States—Juvenile literature.
2. Artists—United States—Biography—Juvenile literature.
[1. Art—Vocational guidance.　2. Vocational guidance.
3. Occupations.]　I. Title.　II. Series.
N6505.G58　1997
702'.3'73—dc21　　　　　　　　　　　　　　　　　　　97-21832
　　　　　　　　　　　　　　　　　　　　　　　　　　　　　CIP
　　　　　　　　　　　　　　　　　　　　　　　　　　　　　AC

Photo Credits:
Page 1: Copyright © Lonnie Duka/Photo Network.
Page 15: Copyright © Margo Taussig Pinkerton/Photo Network.
Page 29: Copyright © T.J. Florian/Photo Network.
Page 43: Copyright © Jeff Greenberg/Photo Network.
Page 57: Copyright © Tom Tracy/Photo Network.
Page 71: Copyright © Bachman/Photo Network.

Published by VGM Career Horizons
An imprint of NTC/Contemporary Publishing Company
4255 West Touhy Avenue, Lincolnwood (Chicago), Illinois 60646-1975 U.S.A.
Copyright © 1998 by NTC/Contemporary Publishing Company
All rights reserved. No part of this book may be reproduced, stored in a retrieval
system, or transmitted in any form or by any means, electronic, mechanical,
photocopying, recording, or otherwise without the prior permission of
NTC/Contemporary Publishing Company.
Manufactured in the United States of America
International Standard Book Number: 0-8442-4382-5
15 14 13 12 11 10 9 8 7 6 5 4 3 2

Contents

An artist is a dreamer consenting to
dream of the actual world.

George Santayana
Life of Reason

Dedication

To my good friends—
Malana Sanders, for so much help in finding people
to interview for this book,
and
Larry Olson, for his patience and support while
I was actually writing the book.

Introduction

You enjoy art. You have a creative imagination. You want the freedom to express yourself and are excited by the opportunity to create and design something new. You have taken some art classes in school and have mastered new skills and techniques. You have gone to art museums and galleries and are inspired by the artwork of others.

Reading this book will allow you to explore many of the different careers available in the art world. Most of the careers will involve creating or working closely with paintings, photographs, sculptures, and other art forms. In reading this book, you'll find out what it is like to have a career as a painter, sculptor, and photographer. You'll also discover what it is like to be an art teacher, member of a museum staff, and art gallery employee. For each of these careers, you will discover what happens on the job, the education and training you need, the pleasures and pressures of the job, the rewards, the pay, the perks, and how to get started now preparing for a future career involving art. Throughout the book, there will be interviews of individuals actually working right now in an art field.

As you become better acquainted with career opportunities in the art world, you will be able to decide if you have the aptitude, skills, and personality to pursue one of these careers. You will also read stories about prominent people and organizations associated with art.

PAINTER

Painters paint the things they see around them. They also paint things that exist only in their imaginations. Some artists paint pictures that do not show any clear subject at all, but instead represent their emotions or ideas. Painters use a wide variety of materials including oils, watercolors, acrylics, pastels, magic markers, pencils, pen and ink, and any number of other media.

1

What it's like to be a painter

Painters usually work independently, choosing what they want to paint and the medium such as oils or acrylics that they wish to use. They may sell their works to stores, commercial art galleries, or museums or elect to sell directly to collectors. Unfortunately, very few painters are able to support themselves solely through their art. Many work as teachers, art critics, salespeople in art galleries, and curators in museums. Some work in totally unrelated fields. Painters generally work in studios, frequently in their own homes. Most will work alone. They typically dress casually and wear a shirt or smock to keep paint off their clothing.

Let's find out what happens on the job

Before painters start their paintings, they often have a sketch of what they want their finished artwork to look like. It may be a drawing that they have made earlier of a scene or object. A painting could be completed in just one session in a studio, but more commonly days, weeks, even months may be required to complete a painting. Some painters concentrate on painting people, which has always been a popular subject. Others paint landscapes, seascapes, and still lifes.

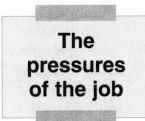

The pressures of the job

There can be considerable frustration in being a painter, especially when you can't put the images you have in your mind down on canvas exactly the way you want them. In addition, finding time to paint may be difficult if you have another job. Nonetheless, if you are working on commission, you will have to create a painting that satisfies your client.

The rewards, the pay, and the perks

How much painters earn depends greatly on the popularity of their work. Such contemporary painters as Andrew Wyeth and Malcolm Liepke earn great amounts of money. Their work is sought by galleries, museums, and collectors, and people throughout the art world lavish attention upon them. Painters struggling to gain experience and a reputation, however, may earn less than the minimum wage for the hours they spend painting.

Getting started

Most high schools offer art classes. Take as many drawing and painting classes as you can. Also, try to take a few art history classes and art appreciation classes, if possible. These classes will teach you the fundamentals of art and painting and help you become familiar with great artists and art.

Internships and summer work experience are also excellent opportunities for young painters. Art museums and galleries are always looking for bright young people who are willing to work and eager to learn about paintings. However, the best way to get started is by actually painting. The more you paint, the more skilled you will become.

Climbing the career ladder

There is no set career path for a painter. Painters tend to advance within the field as their work circulates and they establish a reputation. Entering art shows and having your work critiqued is a helpful way to learn more about your strengths and weaknesses as a painter. It is also important to show your work at galleries and museums and wherever else possible to acquaint the public with your work. Besides gaining a reputation as a painter, some painters also become well-known for their teaching.

Now decide if being a painter is right for you

When you choose a career, you want to make sure that it is compatible with your personality and the type of life you wish to lead. A career as a painter involves working a lot on your own. Does this appeal to you? Can you work well without guidance?

You will often be your own salesperson. Will you be able to be an active salesperson? Can you speak comfortably with people and manage money? Are you willing to look for new opportunities and ways to promote your reputation as an artist? Finally, you will have to be creative. Are ideas for paintings constantly occurring to you?

Things you can do to get a head start

Few artists are able to succeed without some basic training. Art classes at the college level will refine your techniques, expose you to new techniques, and help you learn how to use a variety of mediums. They will also give you the opportunity to put together a portfolio of paintings. This is important when you go to a gallery, museum, or client and wish to have your work considered. Although it is not required for advancement or to help you reach the top quicker, earning a degree in art, art history, or art appreciation will make you a stronger artist as well as give you an appreciation for the skills of master painters.

Let's Meet...

Patricia Krout
Painter

Patricia started painting about ten years ago. She specializes in painting outdoor scenes and mainly paints for clients to their specifications.

What first attracted you to a career in painting?

It was always something that I wanted to do. As I went to a small school I never had the opportunity to take a lot of art classes. In college, I started out as a home economics major but then switched to business. After a few years in the business world, I started taking some painting classes.

What do you like most about your job?

I really enjoy mixing paint colors together to meet a client's idea of what the colors should be for a painting. I also like to attend art shows. This gives you the chance to see what other artists are doing. Also, as a painter, there are many opportunities to try new ideas.

What do you like least about your job?

I don't really like all the cleaning up that comes with painting. It is a very messy career.

Describe your work environment.

I prefer to work outdoors whenever possible. It makes cleaning up a little easier. I have a lot of photographs lying around in my studio. This is because I paint mainly from photos in the winter.

Do you get to meet a lot of new people on the job?

Yes. Painting is very social. There are always art shows, art fairs, or art exhibits going on. People are very friendly.

What is the most difficult part of your job?

It is extremely hard to get the exact image that you have created in your mind onto the canvas. Even with good sketches to help you follow through on your idea, rarely does a painting turn out exactly how you thought it would.

What advice would you give young people starting out in painting?

Take a basic drawing class. The better the sketch that you have before starting your painting, the fewer the mistakes that occur during the creation of your artwork.

Do you work mainly on your own or as part of a team?

All my work is done alone. The only time that I work with others is at art shows or fairs when I am learning new techniques or about new art materials.

A Difficult Work Assignment

It is always hard to please clients perfectly the first time around, according to Patricia. Colors are usually slightly off, or something is not sized perfectly to the rest of the picture. So it is really worth the time to sit down and talk with your clients before you start a painting project for them. A few years ago, Patricia was asked to paint a 4' × 5' painting of a certain landscape scene for a couple's new house. After their initial meeting, she sat down and sketched out a rough picture of the scenery. She took the drawing back to the couple for a quick approval before starting on the actual painting. Halfway through the painting, she took it to the couple and asked for approval again. This time they didn't like the blue color of the ocean and asked if she could please make the ocean greener. After Patricia completed the picture, she brought the picture to their house. The lady thought that the colors were fine; however, she now wanted more in the picture than was originally agreed upon. Since this hadn't been discussed earlier, the lady finally took the picture as it was. Sometimes you must really ask questions to understand exactly what clients want, Patricia has discovered.

Let's Meet...

Marilyn Truitt
Painter

Marilyn travels the world showing her work which focuses on nature. She makes her living as a painter.

What first attracted you to a career in painting?

I kind of fell into it as a child. I really enjoyed sketching and drawing and used to practice sketching members of my family. I took some art classes while in high school and studied under a professional painter for a year before beginning to paint on my own.

Describe a typical day at work.

I usually spend about half of my day in my studio. During this time, I am either painting or making frames. I also frame and mat all my own pictures. The rest of the time, I'm busy ordering supplies, organizing, and doing bookkeeping.

What special skills do you need to be a good painter?

You need to learn to sketch. Once you have a good sketch of an object you can began to build onto it with your painting.

What do you like most about your job?

I like the fun of being creative. With painting you can do your own thing and create the images that you want.

What do you like least about your job?

Getting things ready for a show can be very hectic. You must take a wide variety of pictures when you go to a show because you never know what people are going to like.

Do you get to meet a lot of new people on the job?

You meet people when you go to art shows and art fairs. I also travel all over the nation to attend various types of workshops. This also gives me the opportunity to meet others involved in painting.

What is the most challenging part of your job?

Building art shows. A great deal of planning goes into a successful art show. You must be able to budget expenses carefully to include travel money and entry fees.

What advice would you give young people starting out in painting?

Sketch as much as you can. Then add color. Start with using colored pencils and markers, work your way up to paints. This will allow you to learn how colors come together to create the composition of a picture.

A Most Unusual Workshop

A little more than two years ago, Marilyn had the
opportunity to participate in a really exciting and
challenging workshop in a wilderness area in Wyoming.
The workshop included more than one hundred
painters from all over the United States. They went out
into the wilderness and backpacked for two weeks.
During this time, they also canoed along a river. The
workshop group was searching for animals that they
could sketch such as elk, deer, and moose. Once they
found an animal in a setting that the artists liked, they
would set up and start to sketch. Marilyn has used
many of her sketches to build paintings that she has
shown in art shows and fairs all over the world.
Marilyn found the experience of seeing such large
animal subjects in their natural environment inspiring.

Success Stories

Vincent van Gogh

Although almost wholly unknown during his brief lifetime, the painter Vincent Willem van Gogh is today probably the most widely known and appreciated representative of postimpressionism. Even as a young child, van Gogh showed marked talent. Nevertheless, painting did not become his life's work until after he failed as a businessman and a preacher. His unique style employing intense colors and slashing brush strokes reflected his disturbed mind. Van Gogh suffered from epilepsy. While Van Gogh only painted for a little more than ten years, he was very prolific, producing more than eight hundred oil paintings in the last five years of his life.

Mary Cassatt

Mary Cassatt is probably the best-known female painter in the United States. She became famous for her paintings of mothers and children in everyday settings. Her style employed flat, delicate colors and strong, clear lines that brought a delicate feeling to all her work. Cassatt was closely associated with the French impressionist movement. She was born in Pittsburgh and studied at the Pennsylvania Academy of Arts. Most of her life was spent abroad, where she showed her work with the impressionists.

Find Out More

You and a career as a painter

A painter definitely has to have talent to be successful. At the same time, there are other skills and personality traits that contribute to a painter's success. Study this list in thinking about whether you wish to become a painter:

Personality

1. I can work independently.
2. I love being creative.
3. I am self-motivated.
4. I am self-disciplined.

Skills

1. I can sketch.
2. I have a good sense of color.
3. I have solid business skills.
4. I can see the beauty in an object.

Find out more about a career in painting

The best way to get firsthand knowledge about what a career in art and painting is like is by working during the summer or school year at a local art gallery or studio. It is also helpful to work as an aide for an art teacher. For more career information you can contact:

Carmel Art Institute
P.O. Box 9
Carmel, CA 93921

American Academy of Art
220 State Street
Chicago, IL 60604

National Academy School of
    Fine Art
5 East 89th Street
New York, NY 10128

SCULPTOR

The very first sculptors were people who lived in the Stone Age and carved from wood and bone. The ancient Egyptians cut and polished stone, while early Greek and Roman sculptors used white marble. During the Renaissance, sculptors began to cast in bronze. Today's sculptors use methods and materials far different from those used in the past. Few now carve in wood or stone.

15

What it's like to be a sculptor

Most sculptors consider themselves fine artists. This means that they create art to satisfy their own need for self-expression. They may display their work in museums, corporate collections, art galleries, and private homes. Some of their work may be done on request from clients, but few patrons request specific works to be sculptured. Most sculptors work out of their own studios. Work has to be done quickly because of the expense of maintaining their studios and purchasing tools and materials.

Let's find out what happens on the job

Sculptors create works of art out of materials such as wire, clay, glass, plastic, and metal. Soft materials can be used to make a model that is taken to a foundry so a casting can be made. Sculptors also use such modern equipment as welding tools to cut and shape metal into a sculpture. They may use sheet metal, pipe, and wire and even junk metal from cars to form their sculptures. Modern sculptors also assemble sculptures from ready-made materials such as cloth, nuts and bolts, and gear wheels using drills, hammers, and power tools.

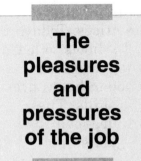

The pleasures and pressures of the job

Sculptors have a chance to show off their artistic talents to a growing number of sculpture lovers. Small works may be shown in homes, museums, or art galleries. Many larger works grace the fronts of public buildings and the lobbies of hotels and businesses. There are even huge sculptures that are too large to fit into buildings.

One of the negatives of being a sculptor can be the high cost of tools and certain materials. Studios can be expensive to maintain, too. Just like painters, sculptors must often show collections of their work at art galleries in order to sell what they produce and to attract commissions. In addition, sculptors may have the additional pressure of meeting deadlines when doing commissioned work.

The rewards, the pay, and the perks

Sculptors are rarely paid in advance for their work. How much they earn depends greatly on the popularity of their work and their ability to secure commissions. Many sculptors, just like painters, are unable to devote all of their time to this career and must hold an outside job.

Getting started

In the past, sculptors always trained as apprentices. Today, many attend art schools to learn sculpture in an environment that lets them spend hours every day honing their skills. The many skills to be learned include: carving, polishing, cutting, molding, casting, grinding, welding, building armatures, and handling trimming and shaping tools.

Climbing the career ladder

Sculptors might advance up the career ladder by taking part in local, regional, and national competitions. However, it is often necessary to have the right credentials, especially for competitions at the national level. This usually means having an art degree of some kind, whether it is from an art school or a college or university. Having works displayed in prominent places can also jump start a career and bring in commissions.

Now decide if being a sculptor is right for you

Below is a list of the qualities a good sculptor should possess. Check off all that apply to you.

— I have the persistence to spend years learning the skills needed to become an expert sculptor.

___ I have the desire to spend a lifetime improving my skills.

___ I have the patience to start out doing simple things until they are as perfect as I can make them.

___ I have the vision to experiment in the use of new materials.

___ I have the creativity to produce truly new works of sculpture.

___ I have the willingness to work with messy materials, in noisy environments, and with heavy and sometimes hazardous tools.

___ I have the essential physical characteristics, which include steady hands and physical stamina.

Things you can do to get a head start

Take art and metal shop classes in high school. Start experimenting with clay, making jewelry, or carving to acquire skills that you will need as a sculptor. Visit as many museums as you can to become familiar with the many forms of sculpture.

Let's Meet...

Douglas Purdy
Sculptor

Douglas has exhibited his sculptures for more than forty years. One of his works, "The Double Eagle," has been accepted into the White House.

Tell me how you got started in sculpting.

I always enjoyed working with my hands, especially modeling in clay. Since my parents were professional artists, I grew up working in a studio. They needed my help and my brothers', so we were able to watch and observe as well as assist.

Did you need any special schooling or training?

Schooling and training can be very helpful. Also, it teaches you discipline which is very necessary. Art school can teach you the fundamentals such as how to use certain materials.

What special skills do you need to be a good sculptor?

Being a sculptor takes many skills. You must have good visual ability (observation of detail). Good dexterity is essential; however, it can be improved with exposure to certain materials. Also, a certain physical ability is needed.

How did you feel when you got your first commission?

My first commission was very exciting. It was a welded wall sculpture to go over a fireplace. It was for a family that had just moved into a new and beautiful home. They were giving me the freedom to create something special for them.

Describe your work environment.

My studio is usually messy. I am an organized person, but in creating the bronze sculptures that I do neatness isn't possible because I have to go through so many steps. I work in clay to create the design, then I make the mold—sometimes using an armature to support it. This involves many different materials. I also use tools for texturizing the bronze and grinding. Since I make my own bases, I need to cut, sand, and stain them before attaching the sculpture. It is not practical to keep everything in order while I am working. I do clean up after every project so that I am able to find everything the next time.

What is the most difficult part of your job?

Creating designs that are unique. I always try to go one step further in each new design so that it is a learning process.

Did you always dream of being a sculptor?

No. It was more of a compelling force— something inside of me needing to come out.

The Path to Becoming a Successful Sculptor

Douglas Purdy was born in New York in 1940. This offspring of two artists has devoted most of his life to sculpture. Working in every medium of metal, he has worked primarily in bronze for the past twenty-four years.

Douglas grew up in Northern California and started designing in his parents' studio while still in grade school. He had an inherent talent which was nurtured at a young age. He worked diligently under the tutelage of his parents, perfecting his designs and learning the art of mold making. After high school, he studied jewelry under a European craftsman and learned the art of chasing (ornamenting metal by indenting with a hammer and tools without a cutting edge), which he often uses in the hand-chisel work on his sculptures. While his designs are contemporary, they emit a classical quality due to the fine textures he chooses to complete his pieces. He makes all of his own molds and meticulously hand-finishes all of his own sculptures. His exciting patinas, which he has developed over the years, add contrast and depth.

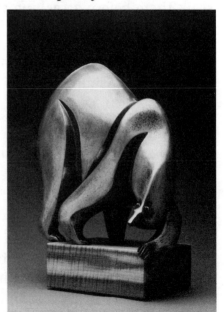

Douglas has exhibited professionally for over forty years and had his own gallery in Carmel, California, before moving to Oregon, where he has established a new gallery.

Let's Meet...

Bill Galloway
Sculptor

Bill produces both large and small sculptures which are exhibited in homes, public buildings, and outside locations.

What first attracted you to a career in sculpting?

I always enjoyed working with my hands and found hands-on projects to be very satisfying. I also enjoyed being able to express myself through my artwork. Since sculpting is not a typical career, it seemed like a challenge.

Did you need any special schooling or training?

I was an apprentice to an older art master for a few years. This is how I learned many of my skills. We worked side-by-side through many projects, allowing me to learn his expertise in the trade.

Describe a typical day at work.

Your work as a sculptor moves extremely slowly. It can be compared to watching a garden grow. You may not see a major change every day, but the final product will be dramatically different from the starting point.

What special skills do you need to be a good sculptor?

You must be able to work long hours and stay focused on your plans for a piece. As in any job, it is important that you believe in yourself and stay true to your initial ideas.

What do you like most about your job?

I really like the fact that my completed artwork is timeless. No matter what happens, my work will always be there.

What do you like least about your job?

My job is very lonely. I am isolated from others. Also, since I work mostly with stone, I am working in an environment with very loud machines most of the day.

What is the most difficult part of your job?

I really cannot turn to anyone to ask questions. If I need help on something, I must sit down and figure out a solution by myself.

What advice would you give young people starting a career in sculpting?

Design skills are extremely important for a sculptor. Whatever you have as a sketch at the beginning of your project will be what you have at the completion of the project. Try to take sketching classes and art classes in school. This will help you to strengthen your skills as an artist.

Putting It All Together—
An Unforgettable Experience

I have had many exciting job opportunities in my career that allowed me to use my creativity in creating a sculpture. However, the most unforgettable experience occurred just a few years ago when I was asked to create a sculpture for the top of the Iowa State Capitol Building.

The entire project was going to be 47 feet in width and 17 feet tall. Since I had all the tools that I needed in my sculpting studio, I did most of the work for the project there. Once all the bits and pieces were completed and only had to be put together, I flew out to Iowa. I completed the remaining part of the project 140 feet up in the air, fitting all the pieces of the sculpture together. It was a gorgeous day, nice breeze, sun shining, and I was on top of the State Capitol Building completing one of my best works ever. The project was an amazing opportunity.

Mount Rushmore National Memorial, a spectacular sculpture in South Dakota, honors four American presidents: George Washington, Thomas Jefferson, Abraham Lincoln, and Theodore Roosevelt. The giant likenesses of the four are sculptured into the granite face of Mt. Rushmore. Washington's head is as high as a five-story building.

The work, designed by American sculptor Gutzon Borglum, was begun in August 1927. Dynamiting was the principal means used to alter the face of the mountain. The first figure to be completed, in July 1930, was Washington. The entire sculpture was not completed until 1943.

The French sculptor Auguste Rodin is one of the most important modern sculptors. He greatly admired Michelangelo and concentrated on the human figure as the famous Italian sculptor did. Rodin modeled his figures in clay and wax rather than carving them from stone. His sculptures show a wide range of human emotions, including passion and suffering. He did not receive recognition early in his career and had to do commercial work designing ornaments for buildings until a large number of artists recognized his genius. You are probably familiar with his most famous work—*The Thinker.*

Find Out More

You and a career as a sculptor

If you have artistic ability and like challenges, sculpture can be a very gratifying career because you are working in three dimensions, which a painter does not have the luxury of doing. However, this is what makes sculpture so challenging. Remember, the most important thing in any form of art is originality. Study the works of the great sculptors to see how each expressed his or her personal genius. Read about the lives of the following sculptors and study their best-known works.

Italian sculptors: Michelangelo, Benvenuto Cellini, Donatello, and Leonardo da Vinci

French Sculptors: Frederic Bartholdi, and Auguste Rodin

American Sculptors: Alexander Calder, Frederic Remington, and Charles Russell

Try to see these famous sculptures in America: Statue of Liberty, Mount Rushmore National Memorial, and Stone Mountain. If you travel abroad, try to see these sculptures: Sphinx, Venus de Milo, and Winged Victory.

**Finding out
more about
a career in
sculpting**

The best way to get firsthand knowledge of sculpting is by starting out doing simple items. Investigate the possibility of working with a master sculptor to learn the many skills sculptors must acquire.

You can learn more about a career as a sculptor by contacting these sources:

American Ceramic Society
735 Ceramic Place
Westerville, OH 43081

The National Association of
    Schools of Art and Design
11250 Roger Bacon Drive,
    Suite 21
Reston, VA 22090

PHOTOGRAPHER

P hotographers use cameras to capture the special
feeling or mood that sells and advertises products,
provides entertainment or decoration, highlights
news stories, or simply brings back memories. With
technical knowledge of how to use camera equipment
and a creative mind, a photographer can turn an everyday item into something visually appealing to the
human eye.

What it's like to be a photographer

You are creative and have a sharp eye for beauty. You also have a good technical understanding of photography, and you always seek the best camera shot. Some photographers sell their pictures as artwork, but most work in a portrait or commercial photography studio. Others are employed by newspapers, magazines, advertising agencies, and government agencies. As a photographer, you will need a lot of equipment, everything from cameras to lights to processing equipment to computers. You may develop and print your own photographs, especially those requiring special effects. This will require you to own a fully equipped darkroom.

Let's find out what happens on the job

You can expect to be fairly active while on the job as you move and shift equipment and objects to be photographed. You may have to carry heavy equipment. The set-up of a photograph is extremely important. You will have to choose the lighting, lenses, film, filters, and camera settings for your pictures. At times, you will have to take many shots before capturing the best image of a product, person, or scene. If you are self-employed, you will need to promote your business and find new clients. You may travel if you work for a publication.

The pleasures and pressures of the job

Being a photographer will give you the opportunity to meet and work with many new and interesting people, perhaps in diverse settings. Whatever field of photography you enter, you will be able to do imaginative and creative work to secure the image you seek.

On the downside, the perfect picture is not always there. People having their pictures taken are not always cooperative. You may have to wait hours for an event to occur. Also, due to the nature of their work, photographers often work evenings and weekends and may have to rush to meet deadlines.

The rewards, the pay, and the perks

The median annual earnings for salaried photographers who work full time is about $25,000. The top 10 percent earn more than $47,000 while the lowest 10 percent less than $12,400. For self-employed photographers earnings depend on the number of hours worked, skills, marketing ability, and general business conditions. Very few artistic photographers are able to support themselves solely through this specialty. Many have full-time jobs in other areas and take pictures on weekends.

Getting started

You are going to need a good technical understanding of photography to succeed in this career. You'll find solid courses at universities, community colleges, and private trade and technical schools. A basic course in photography will cover equipment, processes, and techniques. A bachelor's degree program can also give you the skills needed to operate your own business. You will need to know how to submit bids; write contracts; hire models, if needed; get permission to take on-site photographs at locations normally not open to the public; get clearances to use photographs of people; price photographs; and keep financial records. On the artistic side, you will want to get started developing an individual style that will make you stand out from other photographers.

Climbing the career ladder

Photography is a highly competitive field. The secret to success is to acquire the necessary skills, have solid business ability, and develop a reputation for excellent work. Experienced photographers may advance to the position of assistant, associate, or director of a photography studio. Magazine and newspaper photographers can become photography editors.

**Now decide
if being
a photog-
rapher is
right for you**

Are you the type of person who is willing to acquire the skill needed to succeed in photography? Also, you will need to have the initiative to work independently. Ask yourself if you can work well without guidance. Are you willing to move things around more than once in order to get the best picture? If you want a sameness to your days, photography may not be the career for you as you will be dealing with new people, scenes, and objects to photograph each day.

**Things you
can do
to get a
head start**

Get a basic manual camera. Learn how to use it by taking a class through your local recreational center, park district, or school. Also, try to get a summer or after-school job at a camera shop or a photo studio. You should take classes in school in mathematics, physics, and chemistry because knowledge in these areas will help you understand the workings of lenses, films, light sources, and developing processes. Be sure to take as many pictures as you can to build a portfolio to use when you are seeking full-time employment.

Let's Meet...

Mike Dreas
Assistant Photographer

Mike works as a photographer for a large company doing advertising work. On his own, he does art photography for clients.

What first attracted you to a career in photography?

When I was 14, I received a camera for Christmas. After trying to figure everything out about the camera, I enrolled in a photography class at the local high school.

Tell me how you got started in photography.

As a senior in high school, I was the photographer for the school paper, which helped me decide to major in photography in college. During college, I was the assistant photographer for the school paper and then the editor. In my last year, I received an internship with a newspaper which helped me discover that I liked the commercial and advertising side of photography.

Did you need any special schooling or training?

You do need considerable technical training. This includes learning how to work the various cameras, lenses, and light meters

and knowing the different film sizes. It is also important to know about design and composition.

Describe a typical day at work.

I don't really have a typical day; however, on days when I am in the studio, I clean or fix equipment, tear down old sets, or update my bookkeeping. When I am on a project, I spend the majority of my time getting the subject ready to be photographed. This includes preparing the product (either cleaning or touching up paint spots), setting up the background setting, and getting the film and equipment ready.

What do you like most about your job?

I like the interaction with people. All the people I come into contact with are interesting, creative, and fun to deal with. I also like the constant learning. Since I work with many different clients, I have the opportunity to see and learn about all kinds of products. The satisfaction of creating something that is visually beautiful is something else I like about being a photographer.

What advice would you give young people starting out in photography?

Get a manual camera. This will teach you how a camera actually works. Also, enroll in a basic photography class. A basic class will show you how to use objects in creating your photographs. After taking the class, experiment and have fun.

Creating a Unique Photograph

Considerable thought and planning goes into the creation of an artistic photograph. You must visualize in your mind what you want your final picture to look like and then plan how you will achieve your goal.

Mike once used an old-looking violin as the subject of what turned out to be a beautiful picture. He wanted to create something unique. Using various pieces of photography equipment and the skills that he had learned over the years of being a photographer, Mike began to organize the background setting for his picture and got the violin and other background props ready for the shot. He knew that the lighting and set-up were going to play an important role in the creation of his picture.

Using a special lens, Mike focused the eye of the camera on the label inside the violin. While the label was perfectly clear, the outer edges of the violin were slightly out of focus. This technique made the picture look more abstract and artistic. To add to the picture, he surrounded the violin with pieces of sheet music. The sheet music brought out the real image of a violin. The picture turned out to be one of his best and most creative pieces of work.

Let's Meet...

Tom Eipert
Photographer

Tom is a commercial photographer for a large company who is planning to open his own studio. Currently, he is building his portfolio and collecting equipment.

Did you need any special schooling or training?

You should definitely get a degree in photography. Don't focus on one particular part of photography, but take classes on both the art and communication sides of this career. Also, participate in an internship program, if possible. The more work experience that you can get under your belt, the faster your career will start.

Do you use the knowledge and skills you learned in school on the job?

I use the skills that I learned in school all the time. Actually, they have become second nature to me, and I don't really think about many of them now when I am doing a job.

What do you like most about your job?

I like the casual atmosphere. For instance, I usually wear jeans to work. I also enjoy the people with whom I work. They are very creative, fun, and exciting people.

What do you like least about your job?

I don't like the fact that I have no control over the deadlines of projects. As a photographer, you will often have to work long hours to meet your customers' specifications for a photograph.

Is there a lot of competition for jobs in photography?

You always hear about how competitive the photography industry is; however, once you are in this career you will discover that many of the people who are interviewing for photography jobs really do not have the skills needed to complete a job successfully. As you work your way up the career ladder, you will find that most of the competition has been weeded out.

What do you see yourself doing five years from now?

I am currently working toward owning my own studio. I have started to do some work with outside clients and have been purchasing equipment that I will need.

Describe a typical day at work.

The first thing that I do when I get to work is go over the daily schedule of shots. I also will receive layouts that I have to discuss with a stylist, the person who helps to prep the product and background setting. Finally, I will start shooting various products.

Tom Eipert's Career Advice

If you are truly interested in a career as a photographer, call a studio and ask to job shadow or help out for a day. This will allow you to see what happens on the job. Also, take any photographic opportunities that you can. The real learning as a photographer comes from watching and dealing with professionals in the field. This is where you will learn the most essential parts of photography as a trade. There are many jobs and internships available within this industry, if you just look around. Taking advantage of them will allow you to start building contacts. Not many photographers find their jobs through newspaper ads or "Help Wanted" signs, instead they get them through talking with coworkers and networking through the photography field. A strong portfolio is also extremely important. Your portfolio in this career will act almost like a resume.

Success Story

Edward Steichen was a major force among 20th-century photographers. Born in Luxembourg in 1879, Edward was a leader in the movement to gain acceptance of photography as a fine art. He studied painting in Paris, where his experiments in photographic portraiture led to his recognition early in the century as a photographer of remarkable sensitivity and individuality. For the first few years, Edward chose to specialize in soft-focused photographic images. However, from 1923 to 1938, he was a commercial photographer in New York, where he was chief photographer for *Vogue* and *Vanity Fair* magazines. He played a major role in charge of photography units in both World War I and II. He served as director of the department of photography of the Museum of Modern Art in New York City from 1947 to 1962. In 1955, Edward organized the celebrated Family of Man exhibition that later toured 37 countries. In 1963 he received the Presidential Medal of Freedom.

Find Out More

You and a career as a photographer

Each and every career in art demands different talents from its successful participants. Many of the characteristics and skills of successful photographers are listed below. Check off all that you possess.

__ I have good eyesight.

__ I have artistic ability.

__ I have good manual dexterity.

__ I can work alone or with others.

__ I am patient.

__ I am accurate.

__ I like working with details.

__ I can act quickly to capture a picture.

__ I can help people relax in front of the camera.

__ I have a solid background in mathematics, science, and physics.

__ I have good organization skills.

__ I truly enjoy taking pictures.

__ I am able to recognize a potentially good photograph.

__ I can see the story behind a picture.

**Find out
more about
a career
in photog-
raphy**

Any knowledge that you can gain
to enhance your skills will help
you strengthen your career in
photography. Working in a photography store will give you the
opportunity to learn more about
cameras, the various types of
film, and other photographic
equipment. Work with a photographer in a studio to learn more
about taking pictures. Learn
more about photography as an
art form by volunteering or
working in a museum or gallery.
Find out more about all the
career options in photography
from the following organizations:

Professional Photographers of
      America, Inc.
57 Forsythe Street, Suite 1600
Atlanta, GA 30303

American Society of Media
      Photographers
Washington Road, Suite 502
Princeton Junction, NJ 08550

CAREERS

IN

MUSEUMS

A museum is more than rooms in which valuable objects are displayed, it is a learning place. There are many ways that you can learn about the secrets of the objects that are displayed in a museum. Museums offer classes, tours, movies, brochures, and books. What does this painting mean? Who carved this sculpture? The people who work in museums will have the answers to all your questions.

What it's like to work in an art museum

Art museums are very different in their sizes, budgets, and collections. You could find yourself working in a huge museum like the Boston Museum of Fine Arts, a specialty museum like the Asian Art Museum of San Francisco, or a small museum. In a large art museum, staff members have duties in a finely defined area, such as curator of Egyptian art. However, in a small art museum you will need to act as a "jack-of-all-trades," handling diverse tasks from leading tours to cataloging new paintings and sculptures. Wherever you work, the museum will play an important part in education and culture in your community. Depending on your job, you should expect to work a regular forty-hour week. There are also part-time and summer jobs.

Let's find out what happens on the job

As an art museum director, you will manage all functions of the museum and all the staff members will report to you. If you work as a curator, you will oversee the collections in the museum. You will acquire items through purchases, gifts, field exploration, and inter-museum exchanges. If you are a conservator, you will be an expert in preserving art and will manage, care for, preserve, treat, and document the art in the museum. Exhibits designers make models or drawings of future exhibits and may be responsible for setting up the exhibits, while registrars are in charge of cataloging objects in the collection. Educators are in charge of the teaching programs at the museum, which increase the public's understanding of art. As an assistant, you will assist curators and conservators in their work.

The pleasures and pressures of the job

Being an art museum employee allows you to spend your days working closely with art. Imagine being able to walk by or work with the artwork of such greats as van Gogh, Picasso, and Rodin or promising newcomers to the art world as part of your everyday activities. Since museums depend on money from funding and grants, job openings may be limited and some positions may be cut if money becomes scarce.

The rewards, the pay, and the perks

What you earn as a museum employee depends on the type of job, the size of the museum, and your experience and education level. In 1996, inexperienced curators with bachelor's degrees started at $19,500, while those with some experience started at $24,100. Those with a master's degree typically started at $29,100, and those with a doctorate at $34,300 or higher. A museum director can expect to make anywhere from $60,000 to

$100,000. The median salary of curatorial assistants is $22,500. You can expect to earn more if the pay level is high in the area where you are working.

Getting started

Education is the key to getting a position in art museums. If you want a job as a curator or a conservator, you will usually need a graduate degree plus substantial practical or work experience. Even assistants generally need a bachelor's degree. Some assistants are trained in apprenticeship programs offered through larger museums. Once you have a job, you will need to keep up with developments in the field through meetings, conferences, and workshops.

Climbing the career ladder

Unless you work in a very small art museum, you will need a master's degree to advance. As you gain experience, you can climb the career ladder to curator, to chief curator, and to director in a large museum. Curators in smaller museums often advance to large museums. For many of the advancement opportunities, willingness to relocate often is essential.

Now decide if working in an art museum is right for you

You love art. You may even be a painter, sculptor, or photographer. You are willing to get a master's degree or even a Ph.D. in order to get a job. You have majored in art, art history, museum studies, or library science. You have computer skills and the ability to work with electronic databases. You have taken courses in business administration to gain management skills. You have public relations skills that can be used in raising museum attendance and fund-raising. You are flexible and willing to handle a wide variety of duties. You can handle challenging, difficult tasks. If this description begins to describe you, then a job in an art museum may be the right career path for you.

Things you can do to get a head start

Learn as much as you can about art and art museums. Get in the habit of visiting museums and taking tours led by docents. Attend workshops, seminars, and other museum programs designed to educate the public about art. Because experience is so important, become a museum volunteer or part-time employee. Look for apprenticeships or internships while you are in college to increase your work experience. And be sure to learn computer skills as you will need them for almost every museum job.

Let's Meet...

Holly Day
Curator of Contemporary Art

Holly is a curator at the Indianapolis Museum of Art where she organizes exhibits and travels to find interesting exhibits to bring to the museum.

Tell me how you got started in a career as a curator.

When I was little, my family made frequent trips to art museums. I have always enjoyed looking at and admiring paintings and sculptures. In college, I took an art history course that really interested me and then decided to get a graduate degree in this area.

Did you need any special schooling or training?

Yes, I needed to get a master's in art history. Some curators who wish to specialize in early art history will often go on to obtain their doctorates.

What special skills do you need to be a good curator?

Above everything else, you must enjoy looking at and being around art. Such skills as writing, being able to give talks and lectures without notes, and dealing effectively with people are very important ones to have.

What do you like most about your job?

I like the fact that my job varies every day with no two days ever being the same. I also like the way I'm always learning something new whenever I deal with new artists or exhibits.

Do you get to meet a lot of new people on the job?

My job involves talking with many different people. I spend a major part of my day on the telephone. Since I put together exhibits for the museum, I talk to everyone from the artists who are part of the exhibit to those in charge of hanging the artwork.

Describe one of your happiest moments on the job.

Every time a new exhibit opens successfully is a happy moment. Seeing the public enjoy the art works that you have brought into the museum is a wonderful feeling.

What advice would you give young people starting out a career in a museum?

An art museum offers many different types of careers. Take the time to look for a career that will fit the lifestyle you want. Be sure to enroll in art classes offered through your local museum. Also, attend lectures that the museum offers on various types of art.

The Busy Days of a Curator

Every day when Holly Day goes into work, this curator of contemporary art knows that she is going to be faced with a new and exciting challenge. One of the main things that Holly does in her job is travel to various art museums around the nation to find interesting art exhibits. While traveling, she has the opportunity to talk with artists and learn about their style of work. She then must work with many people at the Indianapolis Museum of Art to bring an exhibit to Indianapolis. First of all, Holly must talk to the funding or trustee department to see if the museum can fund the exhibit. She then speaks with the public affairs department to set up an advertising plan to inform the public about the exhibit. Holly also arranges for the moving of the artwork to the museum and then oversees the care of the paintings upon their arrival at the museum as well as the hanging of the pieces. On the opening day of the exhibit, she will often talk or give a brief summary of the history of the artwork in the exhibit.

Let's Meet...

Rob Lancefield
Registrar of Collections

Rob works at the Davison Art Center at Wesleyan University where he keeps track of the museum's 25,000 pieces of art.

Tell me how you got started in museum work.

As a graduate student in music, I took two art history classes taught by the museum's curator. This deepened my interest in prints and photographs, which comprise most of the Davison Art Center collection. The curator noticed my interest and organizational skills, and saw that I have an eye for detail and handle works of art very carefully. Then the previous registrar resigned, and the job was advertised. I applied by submitting a resume and was hired after a day of interviews.

Do you use the knowledge and skills you learned in school on the job?

Actually, most of the facts I learned in classes aren't applicable to this job! But my education is indispensable for more important reasons. Undergraduate and graduate school taught me to think more precisely and analytically than before, and to strive to write clearly and edit mercilessly.

Describe a typical day at work.

The museum has a small staff, so each of us does a lot of different things. No two days are alike. More than anything else, I work on improving our computer-based catalog of information about our 25,000 art objects. I also do a lot of editing for our publications; help student and faculty researchers find things in the collection; prepare financial reports; do some graphic design for exhibitions; and handle agreements for lending art to other museums and for allowing publishers to reproduce images from the collection.

What do you like most about your job?

I really like working on all different kinds of projects. Although I coordinate my work closely with the curator's needs, often I can focus my energy on whichever of our long-term projects I'm most interested in on a particular day. I might not have so much flexibility and independence at a museum with a larger staff.

What do you like least about your job?

My least favorite aspect of the job is also due to the small size of our staff. Since we don't have an administrative assistant, the curator and I answer general telephone calls; and since my office is the one visitors see first, successive little interruptions can make it difficult to work on projects that require unbroken concentration.

A Challenging Assignment

Recently, the most interesting (and fun!) part of my job has been the making of a Davison Art Center homepage for the World Wide Web. This involves digitally scanning and editing images from the art collection, writing or revising text about the museum, and combining all of this into a pleasing layout. I really enjoyed thinking through how to arrange everything, both visually and logically.

Developing the Web page uses and builds my skills related to graphic design, collections information management, and computers, and even draws indirectly on things I learned years ago when I was studying digital audio recording on my own. It has been a great way to learn how to use the Internet to share information about art. The Web makes art accessible to people who might never visit the museum—or who might decide to do so once they've discovered what they can see at the Davison Art Center.

Netscape: Wesleyan University: Davison Art Center Home Page

Location: http://www.wesleyan.edu/dac/home.html

Wesleyan University

The Davison Art Center

Wesleyan University's Davison Art Center is an active resource for teaching and research, and a museum open to the public. The DAC is one of Wesleyan's principal means of outreach to Middletown and the world.

Success Stories

The Museum of Fine Arts in Boston (MFA), which houses one of the finest collections of art in the United States, was founded in 1870 and opened to the public on July 4, 1876. The MFA's collection covers all areas of Eastern and Western art. Particularly strong areas of the museum's Western collections are the European impressionists and 18th- and 19th-century American paintings, especially those of Benjamin West, John Singleton Copley, and Winslow Homer and his contemporaries.

The decorative and applied arts that are housed in the Museum of Fine Arts in Boston are well represented in a series of period rooms. There is a noteworthy collection of early American silver and furniture and a world-famous collection of textiles from Europe, India, China, Japan, Persia, and pre-Columbian South America.

The Louvre in Paris is one of the largest museums in the world. It has more than 275,000 works of art from almost every period of art and covers more than forty acres of land. It is the home of a number of masterpieces including da Vinci's *Mona Lisa* and the sculptures—Venus de Milo and Winged Victory of Samothrace. The Louvre also has large collections of Greek, Roman, Egyptian, and Oriental antiquities.

Find Out More

You and a career as a museum worker

If you are interested in a career working in an art museum, the job possibilities are far greater than those already discussed in this chapter. Depending on the size of the museum where you work, you can find these museum-related jobs.

accountant
archivist
artist
attorney
audiovisual technician
building superintendent
business manager
clerk
computer specialist
controller
curatorial assistant
editor
electrician
filmmaker
food service manager
gardener/landscaper
graphic artist
guard
historian
instructor
librarian
maintenance worker
model maker
personnel director
public relations specialist
publications director

research assistant
sales shop manager
secretary
volunteer manager

**Find out
more about
a career
at an art
museum**

To find out more about jobs in art museums, especially those actively involved in working in some way with the art collection, the secret is to participate in an internship program or serve as a volunteer. You can also contact the following organizations for additional career information:

Society of American Archivists
600 South Federal Street,
    Suite 504
Chicago, IL 60605

American Association of Museums
1225 I Street NW, Suite 200
Washington, DC 20005

American Institute for
    Conservation of Historic and
    Artistic Works
1717 K Street NW, Suite 301
Washington, DC 20006

CAREERS
IN ART
GALLERIES

F or many individuals, art holds an amazing fascination. They want to be surrounded by art in their homes and offices. And the place they usually go to find works of art is an art gallery, whether they are seeking a photograph of the beauties of nature, a modern painting, a drawing of a clown, or a sculpture to sit on a table. There are thousands of art galleries in the United States.

What it's like to work in an art gallery

There are so many diverse galleries that you can look for a job in a gallery that sells according to your favorite medium, style, period, or artists. Some galleries are just small showrooms in tourist resorts selling paintings and sculptures by local artists; some of the galleries in major cities are huge, selling paintings worth millions of dollars. You could work full time or only part time. You will probably have to work some evenings and on weekends because these are the times that most people shop for artwork.

Let's find out what happens on the job

As an art gallery employee, you are basically a salesperson. You will spend the majority of your time talking to customers, telling them about different pieces of art. You may also spend time hanging pictures and arranging displays. In some galleries, you may also pack and ship items to customers. Gallery owners also spend considerable time working with the artists whose works they regularly display. Together, they must choose which works will be shown and set prices for these works. Time must be spent in looking for new artists, too. This may involve traveling to artists' studios, art fairs, and art shows. In addition, gallery owners are responsible for all the business activities involved in running a gallery, from paying bills to hiring new employees. Time also has to be spent setting up shows and publicizing the gallery.

The pleasures and pressures of the job

People who work in art galleries are typically art lovers. Many are also artists themselves. One of the great pleasures of this job is getting to know the artists who produce the artwork sold in the gallery. You may get the chance to chat with them about their techniques, their work, and even their future pieces. Some of these artists will have already acquired a reputation, while others are just starting out.

There are, of course, downsides to working in an art gallery. You are not likely to work 9 to 5. Art galleries frequently open at 10 o'clock in the morning and may not close until late in the evening, especially if they are located in a tourist area. Most galleries are open on Saturdays and many are open on Sundays, too. Furthermore, if you are a salesperson, there is the pressure of making sales. And if you are an owner, you have to worry about running a successful business.

The rewards, the pay, and the perks

One of the rewards of owning an art gallery is being your own boss. It is also rewarding to plan successful art shows that bring new, exciting artwork to your gallery. When the economy is strong, the demand for artwork is high. How much you earn as a gallery owner will depend on many factors: the size of your gallery, the type of artists shown at the gallery, the area where you live, your expertise in choosing art that will sell, and your business skills. Owner-operators may make between $20,000 to $120,000 a year, with well-known and popular art gallery owners earning even more. Art gallery employees may be salaried and receive benefits or just be hourly workers.

Getting started

Whether you plan to own a gallery or work in one, a knowledge of art is essential. At many galleries, this may mean having at least a bachelor's degree in art history, and for some galleries having a master's degree is required even for entry-level positions. In New York City, competition is so intense at certain well-known galleries that job seekers try to get a foot in the door by working as interns for no wages or by taking the most lowly job available. Of course, for many galleries, having taken art classes or served as an art museum volunteer is sufficient experience.

Climbing the career ladder

If you own an art gallery, you already are at the top of the career ladder. Your main goal then will be to make your business more successful. You can do this by increasing your customer base, upgrading the quality of the artwork you sell, and increasing your sales. If you work as a sales associate, you will be able to work your way up to manager/director.

Here is a job that will allow you to share your love of art with others. Do you have the characteristics it takes to be successful? Check off the skills you possess.

Now decide if working in an art gallery is right for you

1. __ Do you have good people skills? Your dealings with customers are the key to your success.

2. __ Are you adaptable? Galleries must change quickly to meet customer needs.

3. __ Are you knowledgeable about art? You have to be an expert on the artwork in the gallery.

Art gallery owners need these additional characteristics:

4. __ Can you successfully plan events? Part of the success of a gallery is having exciting shows of new artists and new artwork.

5. __ Do you have solid business and managerial skills? They are essential in every business.

6. __ Do you know how to select art that will sell? It is the art in your gallery that will attract new customers and bring back old ones.

Let's Meet...

Mark Ruchman
Gallery Owner

Mark is the owner of an upscale gallery in a suburban setting that has both paintings and sculpture. He holds many shows to introduce new works of art and artists.

How did you know you would enjoy working as a gallery owner?

I enjoy talking with people about art. Whether it's the artist or a customer, it's good to hear the interpretation or reviews on a piece of artwork.

Did you need any special schooling or training?

Yes—in studio fine art. You should have a general knowledge in all areas of fine arts. If you know about the technical skills involved in making artwork, it allows you to talk with potential customers and help them make informed decisions.

What special skills do you need to be a successful gallery owner?

People skills are important. The ability to talk with people one-on-one and occasionally to large groups is essential.

Do you get to meet a lot of new people in your work?

Every day I meet someone new. Whether it's a new artist or potential customer, this profession opens up all kinds of opportunities.

What do you see yourself doing five years from now?

Expanding into new markets. I currently sell to individuals as well as corporate customers. As new homes are built and new businesses open, my opportunities should grow. Also, I'd like to do more consulting work and larger exhibitions.

What is the most difficult part of your job?

Keeping track of everything—finances, inventory, etc. Also, the paperwork is time consuming and moving the shows in and out is a great deal of physical work.

What advice would you give young people opening a new art gallery?

Keep it simple, and watch your overhead. It takes a while to get established in this business, so try and pace yourself. Stay focused on what it is you're trying to accomplish—revisit your business plan.

If you could start over, would you choose a different career?

No, this one has been very good to me.

The Operation of an Art Gallery

Mark Ruchman's gallery has rotating monthly exhibitions, each featuring the artwork of one gallery artist. He will hold a public reception where the public can come in and see a grouping of the artist's work. This generally is done on a Friday night and is called an "Opening." Over the next four weeks, the gallery staff will call customers that they think may be interested in buying this type of artwork and invite them to come and see the show. They call people that may be looking for a painting or sculpture for their home or office.

Mark's gallery represents about fifty different artists. Together with the artist he will select a couple of pieces of artwork from the artist's inventory of works and keep them in the gallery to show customers. Sometimes Mark travels to an artist's studio where a work is created. Other times the artists will bring a selection of works to the gallery.

Let's Meet...

Sean P. Means
Art Gallery President

Sean owns a small art gallery in Peoria, Illinois, where he likes to feature the work of international artists.

What first attracted you to starting an art gallery?

I have always been interested in art. When I moved into this area, I noticed the need for more art galleries.

What do you like most about owning a gallery?

I really enjoy having the opportunity to travel and visit other galleries and gallery owners. You get to meet interesting and exciting people in this job.

What do you like least about owning a gallery?

Having to work long hours in order to fit my customers' needs is difficult. There are times when you put in long hours with no guarantee that you will make a sale.

Is there a lot of competition between art galleries?

Yes, many shops that sell art call themselves art galleries. You must learn how to make your gallery stand out and earn a reputation as a superior art gallery.

Describe your work environment.

I work in a retail gallery setting that is about 1,600 square feet. The walls are covered with artwork, with information about each work posted next to it. I also have a frame shop in the back of my gallery.

Tell me what a typical day is like.

When I first come in, I get the gallery ready to open. This means dusting and arranging the pieces correctly. In the morning after the shop opens, I also do business work and framing because there aren't many customers. In the afternoon, I mainly deal with customers.

What advice would you give young people starting an art gallery?

Think about finances. A great deal of planning is necessary in order to stay in business and remain successful. Look for a good strong market, and have effective advertising.

If you could start over, what would you do differently?

I would not focus on only one type of market. The art industry is an extremely good and strong one to invest in; however, if I have to start over, I think that I would stay more flexible and look into many different types of businesses and opportunities.

Meeting a Well-Known Artist

A few years ago at an art show, I had the opportunity to meet a well-known international artist, Michael Brown. Michael really wasn't an artist who liked to put on art shows. We talked for awhile at the event, and I bought some of his paintings.

After a few months of talking and discussing Michael's unique style of artwork, I asked him if he would do me the honor of giving an art show at my gallery.

I really wanted this art show to be the best ever, so I started advertising early. When the day finally arrived, I had publicized so much that Michael had a group of followers at the gallery to meet him. I also had a television station there to cover the event.

Success Story

Douglas Purdy Gallery is now located on the southern Oregon coast. For eighteen years, it was located in Carmel, California, where the owners, Douglas and Emily Purdy, lived. Douglas, who is today a renowned sculptor, originally exhibited his work in his father's gallery on Fisherman's Wharf in Monterey, California. His welded sculptures in copper, bronze, and steel became so popular that he couldn't keep up with the demand. Soon Douglas was ready to open his own gallery in Carmel, a well-known community of artists, where he had always wanted to be located. Douglas and his wife were only able to afford a 100-square-foot room on the second floor of a very attractive courtyard. Second-floor shops are not considered good locations as casual customers are reluctant to climb stairs. They decorated the gallery inventively on a shoestring using painted coffee cans for light fixtures.

After a few years in the small gallery, the Purdys went together with Robert Davey, a painter, to open a 500-square-foot gallery on the first floor of the courtyard. Emily managed this gallery. In the next five years, Douglas's work became so popular that they were able to become sole owners of the gallery. At the same time, Douglas was able to move from doing welded sculpture to bronze, which he felt was more fulfilling. As Douglas became recognized by collectors all over the world, sales of his work greatly increased, and the gallery became very successful.

Overwhelmed by the number of people moving into the Carmel area, the Purdys moved to Oregon and established a new gallery in 1992. This gallery is located on six beautiful acres overlooking the Pacific Ocean. Not only does this gallery, with Emily as curator, feature Douglas's work, it also has work by nationally recognized artists from throughout the United States. Besides selling works of art, the gallery offers art consultation to help patrons select appropriate pieces of art and also offers personal contact with Douglas.

Find Out More

You and a career in an art gallery

An art gallery owner truly has to be a jack-of-all-trades, especially if it is a small gallery. Look at the following list of required skills, and think about how you would acquire these skills.

1. The ability to select artwork that will sell
2. The ability to recognize promising new artists
3. The technical knowledge of what good art is
4. The managerial skills to own and operate a business
5. An understanding of how to publicize a business effectively
6. A knowledge of accounting and bookkeeping
7. The ability to hire good employees
8. Computer expertise
9. Good communication skills
10. Solid organizational skills

ART

TEACHER

How do you use a pottery wheel? What is perspective? Art teachers have the answers to these questions. How do you make a picture of an apple into a work of art? How do you use color to emphasize parts of a painting? How do you support thin clay figures so they don't fall down? Art instructors at public schools, vocational schools, colleges, and private art schools will have the answer to these questions. Learning about art is fun for everyone.

What it's like to be a teacher

If you are teaching art, you are probably working in a public school. Most of your time will be spent in the classroom, teaching students how to create different forms of art. Or you could be teaching art in a vocational school or two- or four-year college where you may work either part time or full time and your students will be taking classes to prepare for a career in art or simply to learn more about art. There is also the possibility of teaching art classes at a museum, store, or art institute or from your own home.

Let's find out what happens on the job

No matter where you teach, much of your time will be spent on three tasks. At times, you will be in front of your class lecturing or leading your students in a discussion. You will also spend time demonstrating such techniques as sketching and mixing colors. Finally, you will supervise students as they work on their own art projects. This is when you will walk around the classroom, giving individual help to each student. Beyond these tasks, you will have to spend time preparing lessons, grading, ordering supplies, and setting up for each class.

The pleasures and pressures of the job

Seeing a student develop new skills and build on existing skills is always gratifying to a teacher. Being able to share a love of art with students is another pleasure, as is the opportunity to work with students who are highly motivated to learn these lifetime skills.

Teachers always need to learn new skills. There is also the pressure of determining the best way to break a task into steps that students can easily learn and accomplish. In addition, teachers must step back and tell students what to do, not do things for them.

The rewards, the pay, and the perks

Beginning teachers in public schools usually earn somewhere in the range of $24,000 to $28,000, depending on their experience and schooling. The average salary of all elementary and secondary teachers is about $37,000, while the average salary for full-time faculty at four-year colleges is almost $50,000. Full-time teachers at art schools can expect first-year salaries in the range of $22,000; however, well-known artists with an international reputation may earn as much as $60,000. All full-time teachers will enjoy a traditional benefits package as well as some free time for their own artwork.

Getting started

First of all, if you plan to teach art in an elementary school, middle school, or high school, you have two tasks. You need to get a bachelor's degree and to complete an approved teacher training program with a prescribed number of subject and education credits and supervised student teaching. The requirements for teaching licenses will vary by state. Most states will also require license applicants to pass a competency test in basic skills such as reading and writing, subject skills, and subject-matter proficiency. Teachers at two-year colleges can obtain positions with only a master's degree; however, four-year colleges almost always require full-time faculty to hold doctoral degrees.

Climbing the career ladder

Teachers, in general, have short career ladders. After a few years of teaching, art teachers in public schools can become department chairs. At the four-year college level, most teachers enter as instructors or assistant professors. The next step is associate professor followed by the top step of professor. At fine art schools, full-time instructors can become lead teachers. At all levels, it is possible to advance to administrative positions. Many art teachers give private lessons in painting, drawing, and sculpting. How successful they are depends on their reputations as artists.

On the plus side, art teachers are usually working with a subject that truly appeals to them. Furthermore, teachers typically enjoy working with young people. And of course, there are the long vacations that give art teachers time to follow their own artistic interests.

On the other hand, it needs to be pointed out that there are negatives to becoming a teacher. You will not be as well paid as many others with comparable educations. Also, students can be very difficult to handle and may have no interest in your class. Furthermore, teachers have extra duties such as lunchroom or study hall supervision that are not related to what they are teaching. And teachers, like their students, may have homework when they don't get all their work done at school.

Now decide if being a teacher is right for you

Get some teaching experience as soon as you can. It doesn't have to be a formal classroom experience. It could be teaching art to a neighborhood child. Volunteer at school to be an assistant to the art teacher. And if your school has a formal teaching program for students or a club for teachers, participate in them.

Things you can do to get a head start

Let's Meet...

Caroline Mecklin
Art Teacher

Caroline teaches art in an elementary school to students at all grade levels. She tries to improve their self-esteem through her classes.

What first attracted you to a career in teaching?

I was really inspired by some of the teachers that I had. I liked the excitement and energy that they focused on their students and the subjects that they were teaching. Ever since I was young, I have enjoyed helping others. I would give up my study halls at school to help some of my teachers.

Did you need any special schooling or training?

I had to get a degree in education in order to teach art. I think that it is wise to have a double major in art and education so you are truly an expert in art.

Describe a typical day at work.

Since I teach a wide range of students, each day for me is a little different. I usually have supplies that I need to unload and bring into the classroom. A few students come in before class and help me put the chairs down and reorganize the room. Since I like to have things ready for each class as the students come in, I have every student's class folder and materials for the day's project out and ready. The students are then ready for a review of what they learned in the last class and to learn a new skill.

What do you like most about your job?

I really like the challenge of interacting with different types of students. Since all students are special in their own ways, you must adjust your teaching to fit the needs of each one. I also enjoy sharing my love for and talent in art with others.

What is the most difficult part of your job?

Trying to reach out to a student who is bored or unmotivated is a real challenge. It is hard to teach a student a subject that the child is not interested in learning. This is when a teacher must try to become really creative in the methods used to capture a student's interest.

What advice would you give young people starting out in teaching?

I would recommend that they get involved with activities that allow them to deal with people. Young students can babysit or volunteer after school to help teachers. Also, take some extra art classes offered through a local college or museum. This will allow them to see if art is something that they truly enjoy.

A Happy Moment

One of Caroline's third grade classes was doing an art project that involved using glittery fabric to make a butterfly. While each student was working hard to complete his or her project by searching through the fabric to find the right color for the butterfly, she noticed that one little boy who usually worked by himself was helping a few of his classmates. This child, who was usually really hard on himself and had low self-esteem, was suddenly confident enough with his own work that he was now lending a hand to others. Caroline could see the delight in his face as he worked through the assignment making decisions on his own to complete his project. It was clear to her that the boy felt really smart because he was able to pick the right material and put it together to create his butterfly. It was a very happy moment for her to discover how this art project helped his confidence grow. The child had seen that he could complete assignments just as well as anyone else in the class and even be able to help his friends complete theirs.

Let's Meet...

Sonia Kevill
Art Teacher

Sonia is an art instructor whose work combines her artistic abilities with her love of teaching.

What first attracted you to a career in teaching?

Even when I was a little girl, I knew that I wanted to teach. Since I went to a small school, I didn't have the opportunity to take any art classes until I attended college. It was then that I decided that I would change my major to art.

What special skills do you need to be a good art teacher?

You must have an interest in what you are doing. You must like art and be enthusiastic about teaching it to your students.

What do you like most about your job?

I like the fact that I run the art program and have the flexibility to change projects or the subject matter to best fit the needs of my students.

What do you like least about your job?

I don't like the amount of work that I have to take home at night to do. Also, there is never enough time to get everything done in class. Supplies have to be taken out and put back for each class, and a project must be completed in 30 or 45 minutes.

Do you think that you are suited for the job?

Yes. I have a very traditional way of teaching my students. We don't always simply do art projects but also learn about the basic rules and techniques of art and some art history. I think that I work well with my students.

Describe one of your happiest moments on the job.

A teacher is always happy when she sees her students excel at something that they are learning for the first time. Also, teaching students a subject that is dear to me and seeing them enjoy my class is very exciting.

What advice would you give young people starting out in a career in teaching?

You must find a subject that you really enjoy. Teaching requires a lot of dedication. You must want to help your students excel in all areas of school: discipline, listening, communicating, and subject matter. It is also important that you like to be continually learning. As a teacher, you must be up-to-date on all the new techniques that students should know and experience.

An Unforgettable Teaching Experience

Over the years Sonia has come into contact with many wonderful, talented children. However, in one school where she taught, she worked mostly with underprivileged children. They were all extremely talented, she only had to encourage them a little more. The children did all the projects and lessons that her other classes did and never had any major problems.

One day after watching some of the students in this class complete their projects, Sonia noticed how truly excellent the quality of their work was. So she decided to enter the children's artwork into some of the local city art competitions. Almost all of the students received either an award or a certificate for their work. They were all extremely happy and filled with confidence. It was a great feeling to see how proud the children were of their work.

Success Story

School of the Art Institute of Chicago

The School of the Art Institute of Chicago is one of the best-known art schools in the United States. The School was founded in 1866 as a private, coeducational institution and is affiliated with the Art Institute of Chicago (an art museum). The idea of the founding group of artists was to provide an excellent education in the studio arts along with the exhibition opportunities the museum offered. The School has become one of the largest accredited independent schools of art and design in the United States.

Special learning facilities that help students gain a knowledge of artwork include the museum galleries, the libraries, a learning resource center, a film center, a video databank, and a fashion resource center. The School offers a comprehensive college education centered in the visual and related arts.

The main programs of study that the school offers are bachelor's degrees in communication and the arts (including technology, ceramic art and design, design, fiber/textiles/weaving, film arts, painting, photography, printmaking, sculpturing, and visual and performing arts). A master's program is designed for those students who are ready to become professionals in their field or fields. Both graduate and undergraduate students work closely with a faculty of artists and scholars.

Find Out More

You and a career in teaching art

Demand for skilled art teachers is high. Energetic people with good communication skills and a solid education background are needed in schools. Should you be one of these teachers? Think about how you would complete this statement: "I would like to have a job that involves _____." Check the answers that apply to you in the list below.

__ Working with art in some way

__ Teaching art to children

__ Teaching art to adolescents

__ Teaching art to college students

__ Teaching art to adults

__ Teaching art in a public school

__ Giving private art lessons

__ Teaching art at a museum or art institute

To be a good art teacher, you will need expertise in art as well as the ability to make your class interesting, explain things clearly, and build rapport with your students. It also helps to have a sense of humor.

**Find out
more about
a career in
teaching art**

One of the best ways to find out more about a career as a teacher is to follow an art teacher around for a day. By "job shadowing," you can see exactly what a career in this field is like.

You can get information on teaching certification for public school systems from the state Departments of Education. You can also contact the following organizations to answer more questions about teaching:

American Federation of Teachers
555 New Jersey Avenue N.W.
Washington, DC 20001

National Education Association
12012 16th Street N.W.
Washington, DC 20036

INDEX